InfoSearch

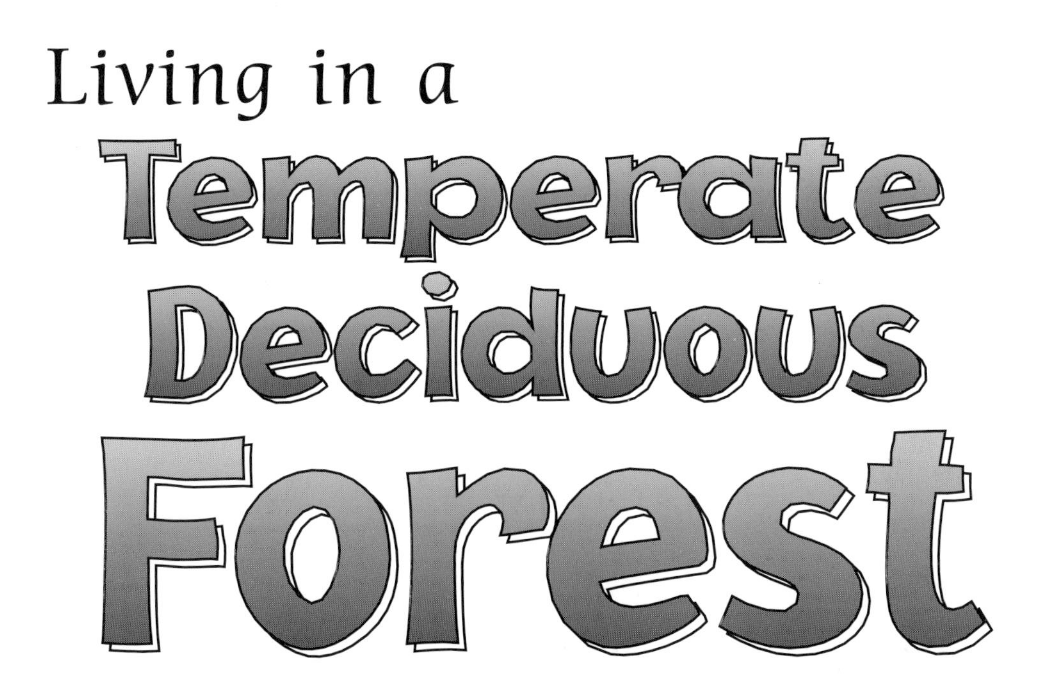

Living in a Temperate Deciduous Forest

Heinemann Library
Chicago, Illinois

Carol Baldwin

a division of Reed Elsevier Inc.
Chicago, Illinois

Customer Service 888-454-2279

Visit our website at www.heinemannlibrary.com

Designed by Kimberly Saar, Heinemann Library
Illustrations and maps by John Fleck
Photo research by Bill Broyles.
Printed and bound in the United States by Lake Book Manufacturing, Inc.

07 06 05 04
10 9 8 7 6 5 4 3 2

Library of Congress Cataloging-in-Publication Data
Baldwin, Carol, 1943-
Living in a temperate deciduous forest / Carol Baldwin.
v. cm. -- (Living habitats)
Includes index.
Contents: What makes land a temperate deciduous forest? -- Why are temperate deciduous forests important? -- What's green and growing in the forest? -- Where do animals live in the forest? -- When are forest animals active? -- What's for dinner in the forest? -- How do forest animals get food? -- How do forests affect people? -- How do people affect forests? -- Earth's temperate deciduous forests.
ISBN 1-40340-839-4 (lib. bdg. : hardcover)
1. Forest ecology--Juvenile literature. [1. Forest ecology. 2. Forests. 3. Ecology.] I. Title.
QH541.5.F6 B33 2003
577.3--dc21
2002011356

Acknowledgments
The author and publishers are grateful to the following for permission to reproduce copyright material:
p. 4 John Sohlden/Visuals Unlimited, Inc.; pp. 5, 18 Rod Planck/Photo Researchers, Inc.; p. 6 Ned Therrien/Visuals Unlimited, Inc.; p. 7 David L. Shirk/Animals Animals; p. 9 Patti Murray/Animals Animals; pp. 10, 15 Jim Zipp/Photo Researchers, Inc.; p. 11 Breck P. Kent/Animals Animals; p. 12 Peter Weimann/Animals Animals; p. 13 M. Hamblin/Animals Animals; p. 14 Stephen J. Krasemann/Photo Researchers, Inc.; p. 16 Charles Melton/Visuals Unlimited; p. 17 Joyce & Frank Burek/Animals Animals; p. 19 Michael P. Gadomski/Photo Researchers, Inc.; p. 20 Gary W. Carter/Visuals Unlimited; p. 22 Michael Pole/Corbis; p. 23 Garry D. McMichael/Photo Researchers, Inc.; p. 24 Jerry Irwin/Photo Researchers, Inc.; p. 25 Thomas Nilsen/Jvz/Photo Researchers, Inc.; p. 26 Kindra Clineff/Index Stock Imagery, Inc.; p. 27 David Muench/Corbis

Cover photograph: Nancy Rotenberg/Animals Animals

Every effort has been made to contact copyright holders of any material reproduced in this book.
Any omissions will be rectified in subsequent printings if notice is given to the publisher.

Some words are shown in bold, **like this**. You can find out what they mean by looking in the glossary.

Contents

What Makes Land a Temperate Deciduous Forest? 4

Why Are Temperate Deciduous Forests Important? 6

What's Green and Growing in the Forest? 8

Where Do Animals Live in the Forest? 12

When Are Forest Animals Active? 14

What's for Dinner in the Forest? 18

How Do Forest Animals Get Food? 20

How Do Forests Affect People? 22

How Do People Affect Forests? 24

Fact File 28

Glossary . . . . *.30*

More Books to Read . . . . *.31*

Index . . . . *.32*

What Makes Land a Temperate Deciduous Forest?

The temperate deciduous forest is always changing because it goes through the four seasons of spring, summer, fall, and winter.

A forest is a large area covered with trees. **Temperate** forests grow in places with warm summers and cold winters. **Deciduous** trees are those that lose their leaves in fall.

Seasons change

Away from the equator, seasons change as Earth moves around the Sun. Because Earth is tilted, the North Pole points toward or away from the Sun at different times of the year.

Temperate deciduous forests are found north of the equator. They are in eastern North America, Europe, and eastern China. In these places, the weather changes through the year. There are four seasons. They are spring, summer, fall, and winter. Each season has different weather. Temperate deciduous forests receive between 30 and 60 inches (80 and 150 centimeters) of **precipitation** each year. The precipitation is spread evenly throughout the year.

Clear sunny days, cool nights, and dry weather are factors that help leaves change from green to other colors.

Trees lose their leaves

Deciduous means to fall off, or shed. Deciduous trees shed their leaves each fall so they can live through the cold winter. In winter, trees can't get the water they need to grow. The water is frozen in the soil. Dropping their leaves allows deciduous trees to become **dormant.** No growth takes place during this time. But in spring, new buds appear and the trees start to grow again.

The leaves of some deciduous trees turn bright colors before they fall. Poplar and birch leaves turn yellow. Red maple and scarlet oak leaves turn dark red. Sugar maple leaves turn bright red and orange. Other leaves, such as hickory, turn tan or brown. Still other leaves, such as willow, stay green until they fall.

? Did you know?

A large maple tree can drop at least half a million leaves each fall. That's enough to make a pile five feet (one and one-half meters) high—taller than you are.

2 Why Are Temperate Deciduous Forests Important?

Temperate deciduous forests provide food and shelter for animals. They also provide many **resources** that people can use.

It takes about 43 gallons (160 liters) of sap to make 1 gallon (4 liters) of maple syrup.

Forests have resources people use

Many trees in the forest grow slowly. These trees, such as oak and walnut, have strong wood. People use wood from these trees for building. Trees from the forest are also used for firewood.

In early spring, people hammer spouts (a spout is like a faucet or tap on a sink) into the trunks of black and sugar maple trees. Some of the tree's **sap** runs out the spouts into buckets. Maple syrup is made from this sap.

Trees and other forest plants make something else that people and animals need. Plants make oxygen and release it into the air. Without oxygen, we couldn't live.

Forests are home for plants and animals

When leaves fall onto the ground, **nutrients** from the leaves go back into the soil. This makes the forest soil very **fertile.** For this reason, many kinds of plants can grow in this **habitat.**

White-tailed deer eat leaves and buds from forest trees and shrubs.

Many animals, such as deer and caterpillars, use the trees and plants for food. Caterpillars eat the leaves of forest plants. Most birds use trees for homes or as a shelter from the sun's heat in summer. Some animals, such as raccoons, live in hollow trees. Others, like salamanders, live under the fallen leaves. Butterflies like the sunny clearings in the forest where lots of wildflowers grow. They drink **nectar** from flowers such as wood lilies and violets.

Forests also get plenty of rain. So, most forests have streams and ponds that provide water for forest animals.

3 What's Green and Growing in the Forest?

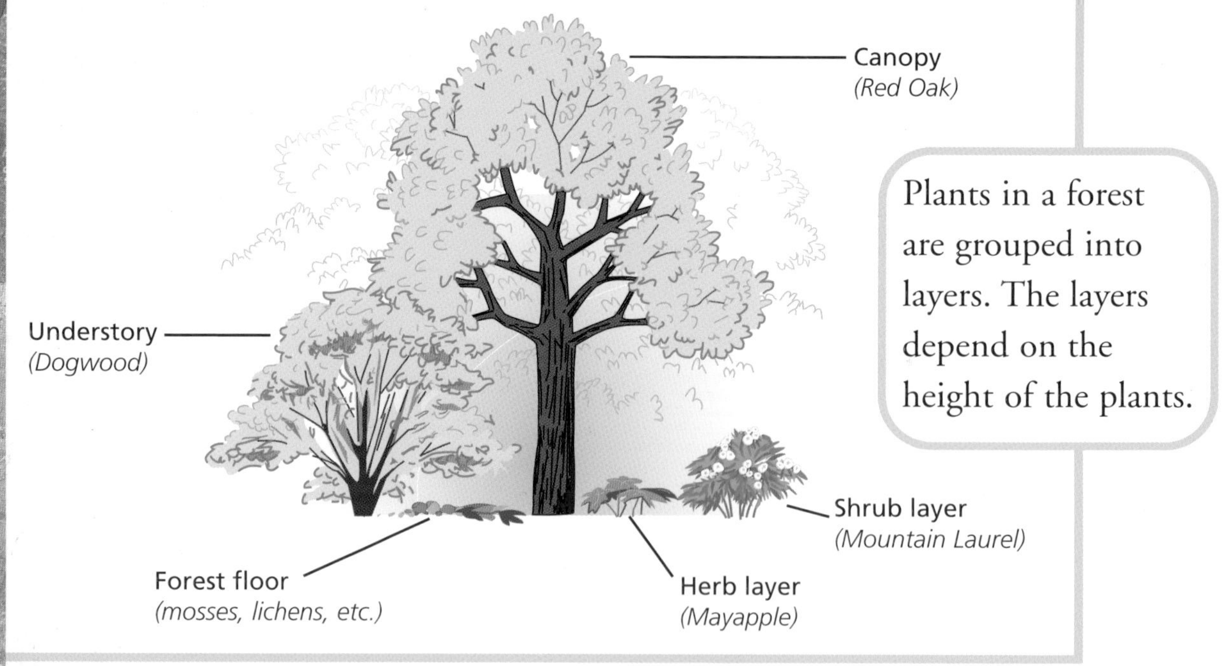

Plants in **deciduous** forests grow in layers. A forest usually has five layers.

Trees

The top layer of the forest is the **canopy.** It is formed by the tops of tall trees. Oak, maple, hickory, beech, and black cherry are some of the trees that make up a forest canopy. This layer filters the light and heat that the other layers receive. However, in many places, sunlight can still reach the forest floor through the trees.

The second layer of the forest is the **understory.** Saplings, or young trees, grown from trees that form the canopy, are part of the understory. The rest of the understory is formed from trees that don't ever grow very tall. These shorter trees include redbuds, flowering dogwoods, and ironwoods.

Shrubs and vines

The third layer of the forest is formed of **shrubs,** or bushes, and vines. Shrubs are plants that are smaller than trees. One shrub has many woody stems. Forest shrubs include mountain laurel, blackberry, blueberry, and red mulberry.

The large leaves of grapevines change color in fall.

Mountain laurel is an **evergreen** shrub. That means it does not shed its leaves in the fall. Deer eat the leaves of mountain laurel year-round. Wild turkeys like to nest under mountain laurels. Birds, squirrels, raccoons, and deer eat the fruits of mulberry bushes. Many forest animals eat blueberries and blackberries.

Vines are plants with long, slender stems. They often attach to trees or shrubs and grow on these other plants. Some grow along the ground. Forest vines include poison ivy, wild grape, honeysuckle, and Virginia creeper.

Wild geraniums have pink or purple flowers and bloom in late spring.

Wildflowers and ferns

The fourth layer of the forest is the herb layer. Herbs are small plants that have soft stems instead of woody stems. Wildflowers and ferns are herbs.

More sunlight reaches the forest floor in spring, before the trees have leaves. So, many forest wildflowers sprout and bloom in the spring. Soon after the snow melts, the forest floor may be covered with flowers such as violets, May apples, trilliums, and wild geraniums. Other wildflowers, such as wood lilies and ground cherries, bloom during the summer.

Ferns have large leaves that grow from underground stems. Ostrich ferns, cinnamon ferns, and royal ferns grow in damp, shady parts of the forests. Ferns produce **spores** that grow into new plants. If you look at the underside of a fern leaf, you might see little brown dots. Each of these dots holds many spores.

? Did you know?

When the seedpods of wild geraniums get ripe and pop open, they can shoot seeds more than 30 feet (9 meters) into the air.

Mosses and lichens

The forest floor makes up the fifth layer of the forest. Mosses and lichens grow on soil and rocks on the forest floor. Some also grow on tree trunks. Fallen leaves and soil also make up part of the bottom forest layer.

Mosses are tiny plants without leaves, stems, or roots. Food and water move slowly through the moss plants from one **cell** to the next. If mosses were large plants, they would dry out before water could get to the tops of the plants. For this reason, mosses are small.

A lichen is made of an **alga** and a **fungus.** They live together as partners. The alga makes food for itself and the fungus. The fungus gets water and minerals for the alga. Lichens often form brightly colored patches on rocks and tree trunks.

Several different mosses often grow together in patches on the forest floor.

4 Where Do Animals Live in the Forest?

Animals live in every level of the forest. Many move about through the different layers.

Animals live in trees and shrubs

Most forest birds, such as jays, chickadees, and woodpeckers, build their nests in trees or shrubs. There, they feed on seeds, berries, and insects. Porcupines are good climbers and spend most of their time in trees. Gray squirrels and raccoons build nests in holes in forest trees. Door mice live in thick bushes.

Only bear cubs are light enough to climb trees.

Animals live on the ground

Wild boars, brown bears, and red deer live in the forests of Europe. They spend all their time on the ground. In North American forests, you might see wild turkeys, red foxes, and whitetail deer walking about. Opossums live on the ground, but they climb trees to escape their enemies.

Eurasian badgers live in a family group in underground burrows with many rooms.

Some animals live on the ground among the fallen leaves and under logs. If you look closely, you might see many different kinds of insects such as beetles and ants. You might also find slugs, which are snails without shells.

Animals live underground

Some animals live in **burrows** all the time. Others spend only part of their time there. Eurasian badgers spend their days underground, but come out at night to hunt for earthworms. There are usually hundreds of earthworms under every square yard of the forest. Earthworms move through the forest soil, feeding on decaying plant matter.

Chipmunks are ground animals, but they spend part of their lives in burrows. They use them as winter homes. They also use them to escape from foxes, hawks, or raccoons. Female chipmunks also use the burrows as dens for their young.

5 When Are Forest Animals Active?

Wild turkeys feed on acorns, nuts, berries, seeds, and insects at dawn and dusk.

Animals that live in **temperate deciduous** forests are **adapted** to living in the forest. Different animals are adapted in different ways.

Some animals are active during the day

Animals such as butterflies, chipmunks, and most birds are active during the day. These animals are **diurnal.** Daylight makes it easier for some animals to find food. But it also makes it easier for **predators** to find and eat them. Many hawks perch in trees or fly high in the sky to look for food. They couldn't do this at night.

Some animals are active at dawn and dusk

Animals that are active at dawn and dusk are called **crepuscular.** Porcupines feed at dawn and dusk. They eat mainly tree buds and bark. Deer, brown bears, and wild turkeys are also crepuscular.

Most owls hunt at night. Their large eyes help them see well in the dark. This is a great horned owl.

Some animals are active at night

Many forest animals are **nocturnal.** They are active only at night. Many nocturnal animals, such as owls and bobcats, have a special structure in their eyes for seeing better at night. This structure makes their eyes glow in the dark.

Some nocturnal animals, such as raccoons and foxes, have a better sense of smell than diurnal animals. They often find their way to food by following their noses. Raccoons also use their sense of touch to find food in the dark. They can find fish by feeling around in shallow forest streams. Foxes do not like to hunt during the day. But if they are hungry enough or have babies to feed, they will.

At night, the forest is usually quieter, and sounds travel a long way. Some nocturnal animals, such as rabbits, have big ears. This helps them hear predators that might want to eat them and gives them time to escape.

Flowers that hummingbirds feed on don't bloom in winter, so they must migrate to find food. This is a ruby-throated hummingbird

Some animals sleep through winter

Some forest animals **hibernate** through cold winters. A hibernating animal goes into a deep sleep. It's breathing rate, heart rate, and body temperature are greatly reduced. To get ready for winter, it eats large amounts of food. It will use stored body fat as food. A **burrow** protects it from the cold. A groundhog is an animal that hibernates.

Some animals move to a warmer place

In fall, some forest birds **migrate** to warmer places to escape the cold winter. Ruby-throated hummingbirds leave the forests of eastern North America. They fly to Central America to spend the winter. In spring, they return north.

Some bats migrate and then hibernate. In winter, there are no insects for little brown bats to eat, so the bats fly south. Then they gather in groups in caves or other protected places. There, they spend the winter hibernating.

Some animals are active year round

Some animals don't migrate or hibernate. These animals must find food and water throughout the year.

Squirrels bury nuts in the fall. Then they dig them up in winter when they cannot find other food. Nuts that they don't dig up may grow into new trees.

Unlike squirrels, deer don't store food for winter. They eat what they can find. If there is only a little snow on the ground, deer can uncover moss, leaves, and acorns with their hooves. If the snow is deep, they eat twigs and branches from trees such as birch and willow.

Red foxes must hunt for food all year long. Fur between their toes keeps their feet warm when they hunt in winter. The fur also keeps them from slipping when running over ice or snow.

Red foxes listen for the sounds of mice tunneling under the snow. This fox is about to pounce on a mouse.

6 What's for Dinner in the Forest?

Ferns grow in shady places in the forest.

All life, in all **habitats,** begins with plants. Animals eat the plants. Other animals eat the plant-eaters.

Plants

Plants make, or produce, their own food. They are called **producers.** Trees, shrubs, flowers, ferns, and mosses are producers that grow in forests. They make food from carbon dioxide gas in the air and water from their roots. Plants need energy to change the carbon dioxide and water into sugars. The energy comes from sunlight. This process is called **photosynthesis.**

Other producers

Not all producers are plants. **Algae** belong to a group of living things called **protists.** In lichens, the algae are the producers. They make food for themselves and the **fungi** they live with.

Bracket fungus grows on all kinds of dead wood.

Animals

Animals are called **consumers** because they eat, or consume, food. Some forest animals, such as deer, rabbits, and caterpillars, eat only plants. These animals are called **herbivores.** Other animals, such as skunks and wild turkeys, eat both plants and animals. They are called **omnivores.** Still others, such as gopher snakes and bobcats, eat only animals. They are called **carnivores.**

The clean-up crew

Other kinds of consumers feed on dead plants and animals and their waste. They are called **decomposers. Bacteria, fungi,** and some beetles are decomposers. Without them, dead plants and animals would pile up everywhere.

Fungi grow right into their food by spreading webs of thin strands. These strands reach into dead leaves, branches, logs, and dead animals. You don't usually see this part of a fungus. But you can see another part. Mushrooms growing in forests are the top parts of fungi.

7 How Do Forest Animals Get Food?

Barred owls hunt and eat mice, birds, other small animals.

Some animals hunt other animals. Other animals **scavenge** or **forage.**

Hunting

Animals that hunt and kill other animals for food are **predators.** Bobcats are predators. They chase down and eat rabbits and birds. Gray squirrels eat seeds, acorns, and nuts. But they also hunt and eat insects. So they are also predators. Animals that predators eat are called **prey.** Insects are prey of squirrels and skunks. Mice are prey of barred owls.

Some forest animals are both predators and prey. Chickadees are small birds that eat caterpillars. This means they are predators. However, chickadees are also eaten by hawks and owls. So, they are also prey.

Foraging

Some animals, such as deer, rabbits, and European bison, are foragers. They move about to search for food. They search for grasses, buds, leaves, and twigs to eat.

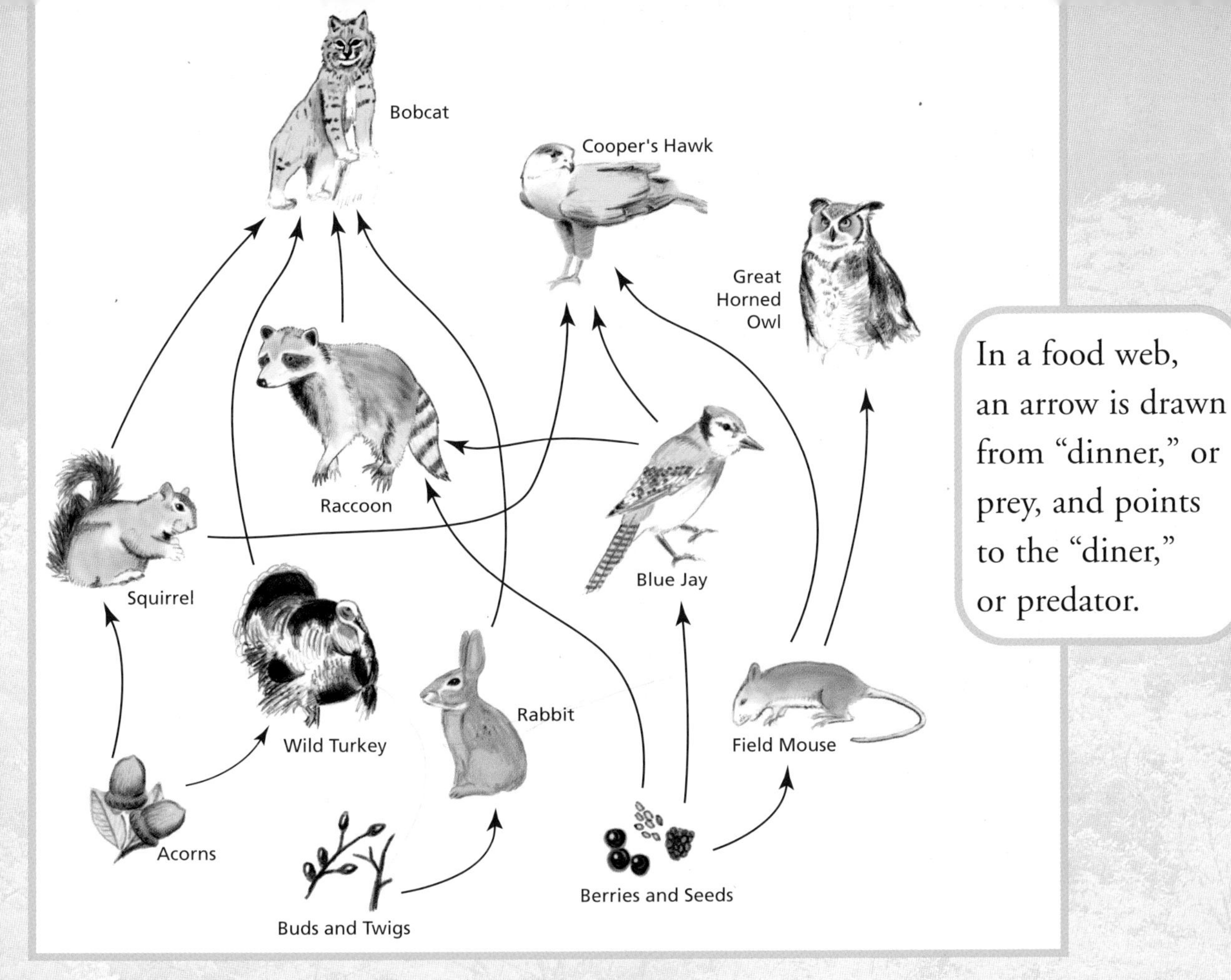

In a food web, an arrow is drawn from "dinner," or prey, and points to the "diner," or predator.

Scavenging

Some insects are forest scavengers. Scavengers are animals that eat the bodies of animals or plants that are already dead. Purple emperor butterflies drink liquids from the bodies of rotting animals. Stag beetles eat rotting trees.

Planning the menu

The path that shows who eats what is a **food chain.** All living things are parts of food chains. In North American forests, bluejays eat seeds. Raccoons eat young bluejays. And bobcats eat raccoons. Another forest food chain includes berries, mice, and owls. All the food chains that are connected in a forest make up a **food web.**

8 How Do Forests Affect People?

Furniture, such as chairs, is made from the wood of a tree.

Plants and animals are not the only living things that use forests. People also need forests.

Forests provide jobs for people

Many people who live in or near forests have jobs that depend on the forests' trees.

Loggers cut trees from forest lands. The branches are trimmed off, and then logs are loaded onto big trucks. Drivers take the logs to sawmills. There, workers cut the logs into lumber. Workers use the lumber to make floors, buildings, and furniture.

Other workers who depend on forests include foresters, game wardens, and guides. Foresters help decide the best ways to use and protect forests. Game wardens make sure that people follow laws that protect the plants and animals in the forest. Guides help people find things in the forest. They might help people find and take pictures of eagles or other birds.

Forest fires destroy homes and businesses

Most forest fires are started by lightning. However, people start some fires. **Deciduous** forests are often too damp to let fires spread easily. But during a **drought,** the forest can become dry enough to burn.

In a forest, fire is nature's way of getting rid of dead wood and plant litter. After a fire, there's more space for young trees to grow. More sunlight reaches the forest floor. This allows many new, small plants to grow.

However, when people build homes and businesses in the forest, fires can destroy them. The thick bark of an oak tree protects it from the heat of a forest fire. Houses and other buildings aren't so lucky.

Fires can help the forest. But they can destroy buildings in the forest.

9 How Do People Affect Forests?

This land was once covered by a forest.

People often harm forests. But today, many people are working to protect forests.

People cut many trees

People started cutting down **temperate** forests thousands of years ago to make farmland. Much of what used to be temperate forest in Europe and the eastern United States is farmland today.

When people cut too many trees, animals lose food and shelter. Without tree roots to hold soil in place, the soil washes away. Soil that took thousands of years to form can be lost in a few years. Without the **fertile** soil, new trees and other plants can't grow.

? Did you know?

In 1919, the European bison died out in the wild because of hunting and cutting down of forests. Offspring from zoo animals were released into the wild. Now more than 500 wild bison live in the forests of Europe.

People build homes in forests

Many cities and towns were built on land that once was forest. Before 1800, forests covered most of the state of Ohio. Today, only 15 out of every 100 acres (7 out of 40 hectares) in Ohio is forest. People build roads and homes in forests, and this destroys the **habitat.** Large **predators,** such as wolves, bears, and mountain lions, no longer live in some parts of the United States.

Pollution harms forest plants and animals

Many temperate forests in North America and Europe are being harmed by **pollution.** Acid rain kills millions of trees. The pollution can come from factories hundreds of miles away. It is carried by wind and rain to the forests.

Acid rain has harmed many of the forests in New England.

People use forests for recreation

Many people look forward to spending time in forests. Some just enjoy a quiet walk in the woods. They might spend time watching birds or looking at wildflowers in the spring.

Other people like to go camping in the forest. Some camp in tents and cook over a campfire. Others camp in motor homes. But all campers seem to like getting away from cities and spending time in the forest **habitat.**

Some people spend their vacations at cabins in forests. They may hunt in forests or fish in the forests' lakes and streams. Others may hike through the woods.

Many forests have trails through them. People can ride bikes or horses on these trails in warm weather. In winter, many trails are used by cross-country skiers or people who ride snowmobiles.

Many people enjoy camping and hiking in the forests.

In Shenandoah National Park, Virginia, the forest habitat is protected.

People protect forests

Conservation is the careful use of **resources** so that they will last longer. People have learned that forest conservation is important. Many forests are now protected from overcutting. Removing older trees allows young trees to grow faster and straighter. Sometimes new trees are planted. New trees grow fairly quickly because the forest soil is **fertile.**

In some countries, governments have laws that protect some parts of the forests. In the United States, the Forest Service decides which parts of national forests can be cut and which parts cannot. Other forests are protected because they are state or national parks.

Private groups like The Nature Conservancy also work with states to protect forests. The National Audubon Society maintains a number of protected forest areas and runs education centers all over the United States.

Forests are important, beautiful, and peaceful places.

Fact File

Forests of the World

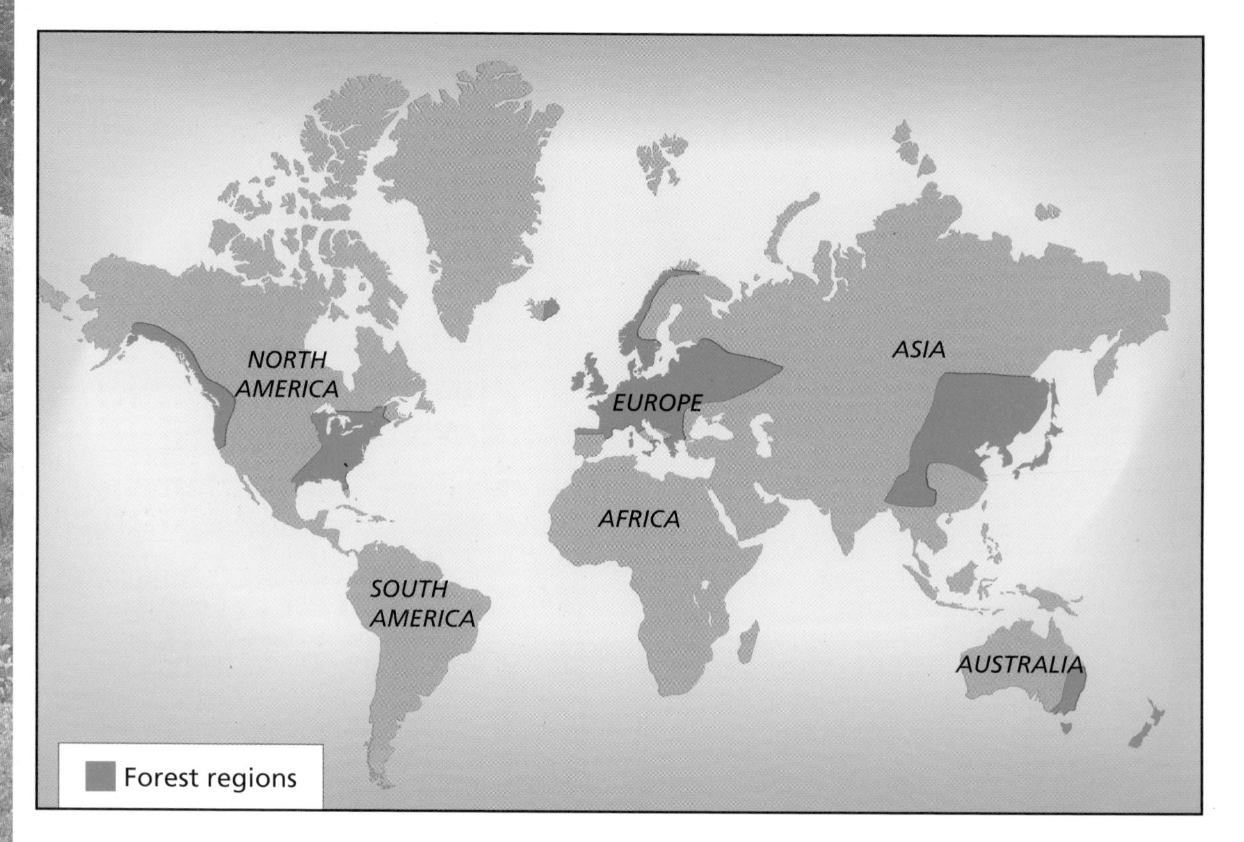

The green areas on the map show all the places where temperature deciduous forests can grow. In these areas, the weather and the soil conditions are right for this type of forest. But in Europe and eastern North America, much of the forest has been replaced by farmland.

Forest Trees

Name	Height*	Importance
downy serviceberry	Up to 40 feet	Bears, squirrels, and bears feed on the red fruits; deer eat the leaves and twigs.
American beech	Up to 100 feet	Nuts are eaten by squirrels, chipmunks, black bears, turkeys, and grouse.
eastern hop hornbeam	25 to 40 feet	Deer eat the leaves and twigs; birds and squirrels eat the seeds and buds.
wild black cherry	Up to 100 feet	Birds and small animals eat the fruit; wood is used to make furniture.
sweet birch	Up to 60 feet	Birds eat the seeds; deer and porcupines eat the leaves and twigs; used as lumber.
white oak	Up to 115 feet	Acorns are eaten by deer, raccoons, squirrels, and turkeys; wood is used for building houses, furniture, and floors.
northern red oak	60 to 80 feet	Insects, deer, black bears, raccoons, squirrels, turkeys, and bluejays eat the acorns; deer eat the buds and young twigs in winter; wood is used for flooring and furniture.
sugar maple	Up to 100 feet	Birds and small animals eat the seeds; deer eat leaves, buds, and twigs; squirrels and porcupines eat tips of small branches; sap is used to make maple syrup; wood is used to make furniture.
shagbark hickory	Up to 150 feet	Nuts from this tree were an important food to Native Americans and early settlers; squirrels eat nuts; wood is used to smoke meats and to make tool handles.
butternut	Up to 100 feet	Nuts are eaten by squirrels, rabbits, and deer; wood is used to make boxes.
white ash	80 to 100 feet	Turkeys, quail, and songbirds eat the seeds; wood is used to make tool handles and baseball bats.

*10 feet (3 meters) = 1 story of a building

Glossary

adapted changed to live under certain conditions

alga (plural: **algae**) tiny li[illegible] its own fo[illegible]

bacteria livi[illegible] except wit[illegible] decompose[illegible]

burrow hole [illegible] shelter

canopy coveri[illegible]

carnivore anim[illegible]

cell smallest un[illegible] things are ma[illegible]

conservation ca[illegible] they will last lo[illegible]

consumer living t[illegible] plants for food

crepuscular active at dawn and dusk

deciduous shedding leaves at particular season

decomposer consumer that puts nutrients from dead plants and animals back into the soil, air, and water

diurnal active during the day

dormant state of rest; not active

drought long time without rain

evergreen having green leaves or needles all year long

fertile able to produce crops or other plants easily

food chain path that shows who eats what in a habitat

food web group of connected food chains in a habit[illegible]

[illegible]nder about in search of food

[illegible]ural: **fungi**) living thing that feeds on [illegible]iving plant or animal matter. [illegible]ns and molds are fungi.

[illegible]e where a plant or animal naturally [illegible]

[illegible]imal that eats only plants

[illegible]end the winter in a state in which [illegible] breathing, heart rate, and body [illegible] is greatly reduced

[illegible] from one place to another with [illegible]f seasons

[illegible]liquid found in flowers

nocturnal active at night

nutrient material that is needed for the growth of a plant or animal

omnivore animal that eats plants and animals

photosynthesis process by which green plants trap the sun's energy and use it to change carbon dioxide and water into sugars

pollution harmful materials in the water, air, or land

precipitation rain, snow, sleet, or hail

predator animal that hunts and eats other animals

prey animal that is hunted and eaten by other animals

producer living thing that can use sunlight to make its own food

protist type of living thing that is neither a plant nor an animal. Algae are protists.

Glossary

resource anything that provides something that people, plants, or animals need

sap liquid that moves through tubes in trees and some other plants

scavenge feed on the bodies of dead animals

scavenger animal that eats the bodies of animals that are already dead

shrub plant smaller than a tree with many separate wood stems that start near the ground

spore tiny cell that can grow into a new living thing

temperate has warm or hot summers and cool or cold winters

understory forest layer formed by young trees and small trees

More Books to Read

Fielding, Eileen. *The Eastern Forest*. Salt Lake City, Utah: Benchmark Books, 1999.

Fink Martin, Patricia A. *Woods and Forests*. Danbury, Conn.: Franklin Watts, 2000.

Johnson, Rebecca L. *A Walk in the Deciduous Forest*. Minneapolis, Minn.: Carolrhoda Books, 2001.

Woodward, John. *Temperate Forests*. Austin, Tex.: Raintree/Steck Vaughn, 2002.

Index

acid rain 25
algae 11, 18
animals 7, 9, 12–17, 19, 20, 21, 24, 25

bacteria 19
bats 16
beetles 19, 21
birds 7, 12, 16
bison 24
burrows 13, 16

canopy 8
carnivores 19
conservation 27
consumers 19
crepuscular animals 14

deciduous forests 4, 5, 8, 23
decomposers 19
deer 17
diurnal animals 14
dormancy 5
droughts 23

earthworms 13
European bison 24
evergreen shrubs 9

fall 4, 5, 9
farming 24
ferns 10
fires 23
firewood 6
floor 11
food 13, 15, 18, 24
food chain 21
food web 21
foragers 20
forest fires 23
foresters 22
fungi 11, 18, 19

game wardens 22
geraniums 10
guides 22

herb layer 10
herbivores 19
hibernation 16

insects 13, 16, 19, 20, 21

leaves 4, 5, 7, 9, 10, 11, 12, 13, 19, 20
lichens 11, 18
loggers 22
lumber 6, 22

maple syrup 6
maple trees 5
migration 16
mosses 11

National Audubon Society 27
Nature Conservancy 27
nocturnal animals 15
nutrients 7

omnivores 19
oxygen 6

photosynthesis 18
plants 4, 5, 6, 7, 8–11, 18, 22, 23, 24, 27
pollution 25
precipitation 4, 7, 25
predators 14, 15, 20, 25
producers 18
protists 18

rain 4, 7, 25
recreation 26
red foxes 17
resources 6, 27

sap 6
saplings 8
scavengers 20, 21
seasons 4, 5, 9, 10, 16
shrubs 7, 9, 12, 18
slugs 13
soil 7, 11, 13, 24, 27
spores 10
spouts 6
spring 4, 5, 10
squirrels 17
summer 4
sunlight 8, 10, 23

temperate deciduous forests 4, 6, 14, 24

understory 8
United States Forest Service 27

vines 9

wildflowers 7, 10
winter 4, 5, 16